BODY SYSTEMS

The Respiratory System

by Kay Manolis

Consultant:
Molly Martin, M.D.
Internal Medicine
MeritCare, Bemidji, MN

BELLWETHER MEDIA • MINNEAPOLIS, MN

Note to Librarians, Teachers, and Parents:

Blastoff! Readers are carefully developed by literacy experts and combine standards-based content with developmentally appropriate text.

Level 1 provides the most support through repetition of high-frequency words, light text, predictable sentence patterns, and strong visual support.

Level 2 offers early readers a bit more challenge through varied simple sentences, increased text load, and less repetition of high-frequency words.

Level 3 advances early-fluent readers toward fluency through increased text and concept load, less reliance on visuals, longer sentences, and more literary language.

Level 4 builds reading stamina by providing more text per page, increased use of punctuation, greater variation in sentence patterns, and increasingly challenging vocabulary.

Level 5 encourages children to move from "learning to read" to "reading to learn" by providing even more text, varied writing styles, and less familiar topics.

Whichever book is right for your reader, Blastoff! Readers are the perfect books to build confidence and encourage a love of reading that will last a lifetime!

This edition first published in 2009 by Bellwether Media, Inc.

No part of this publication may be reproduced in whole or in part without written permission of the publisher. For information regarding permission, write to Bellwether Media, Inc., Attention: Permissions Department, Post Office Box 19349, Minneapolis, MN 55419.

Library of Congress Cataloging-in-Publication Data
Manolis, Kay.
  Respiratory system / by Kay Manolis.
    p. cm. – (Blastoff! readers: body systems)
  Includes bibliographical references and index.
  Summary: "Introductory text explains the functions and physical concepts of the respiratory system with color photography and simple scientific diagrams. Intended for students in grades three through six"–Provided by publisher.
  ISBN-13: 978-1-60014-246-8 (hardcover : alk. paper)
  ISBN-10: 1-60014-246-X (hardcover : alk. paper)
  1. Respiratory organs–Juvenile literature. I. Title.
  QP121.M28 2009
  612.2–dc22   2008032702

Contents

What Is the Respiratory System?

Make a wish and blow out the candles! Your respiratory system makes this possible. This system moves air into and out of your body. The respiratory system takes **oxygen** from the air when you breathe in. It moves **carbon dioxide** out of your body when you breathe out.

Oxygen Goes In

Your body is made up of billions of **cells**. You have muscle cells, brain cells, and many other kinds of cells. Every cell needs oxygen to work.

Oxygen is in the air. Your respiratory system takes oxygen from the air and moves it into cells where it can be used.

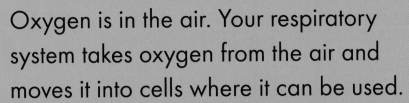

fun fact

An adult doing normal activities takes between 12 to 20 breaths a minute. That adds up to more than 20,000 breaths in a day!

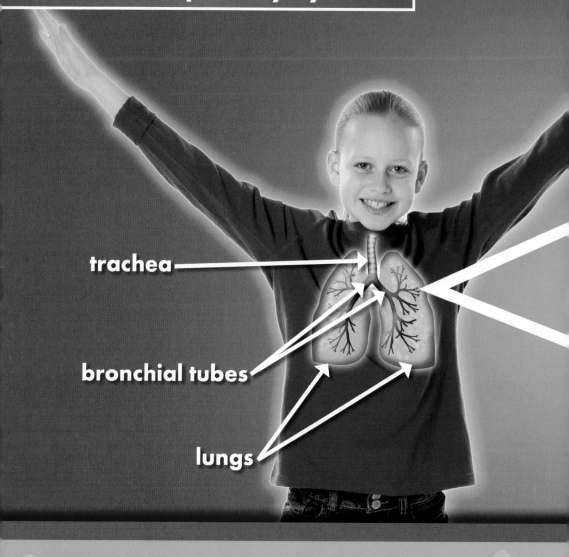

trachea

bronchial tubes

lungs

When you breathe in, air travels through several parts of the respiratory system. It enters the nose or mouth. It passes through the **trachea**, which branches into two **bronchial tubes**. Each tube leads to one of the **lungs**.

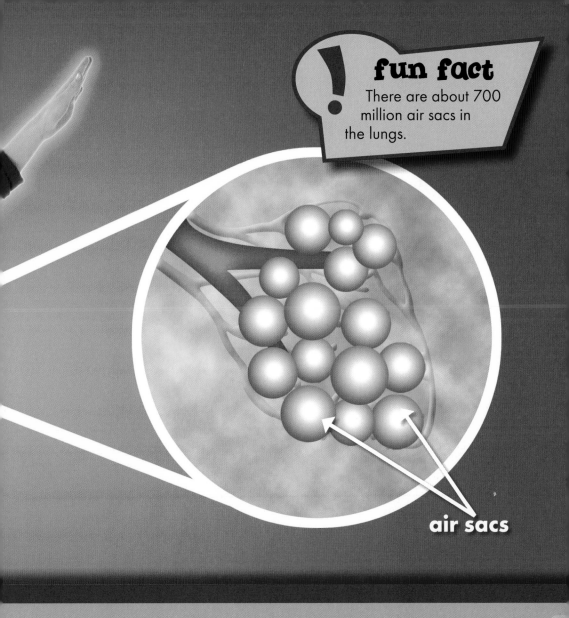

air sacs

In the lungs, these tubes branch into even smaller tubes. At the end of the smallest tubes are millions of tiny **air sacs**, like bunches of balloons. The air fills these air sacs.

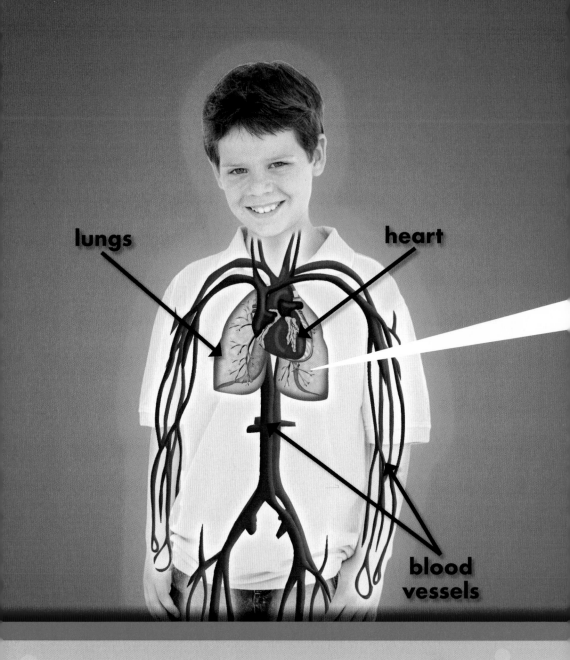

lungs

heart

blood
vessels

The respiratory system works with the body's
circulatory system. This includes the
heart, blood, and **blood vessels** that carry
blood throughout the body.

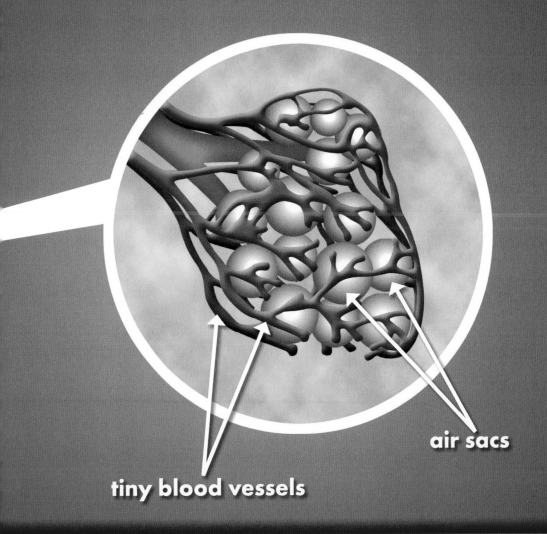

air sacs

tiny blood vessels

Tiny blood vessels cover the air sacs in the lungs. Oxygen moves out of the air sacs into the blood vessels. The heart pumps this oxygen-filled blood to the rest of the body.

Oxygen Flows with Blood

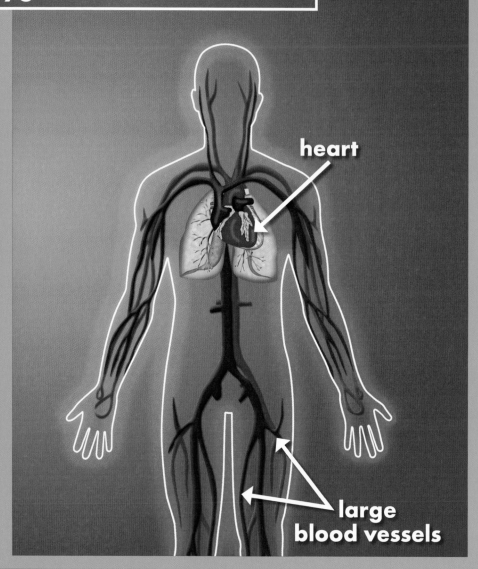

heart

large blood vessels

Oxygen-filled blood from the heart and lungs is pumped into large blood vessels. These large blood vessels branch into smaller vessels throughout the body.

As blood moves through small vessels, oxygen leaves the blood and enters cells. Oxygen helps cells get the energy they need to work.

Carbon Dioxide Goes Out

As cells work, they produce carbon dioxide, which the body does not need. The carbon dioxide moves out of cells and into blood. Blood carries carbon dioxide back to the lungs. There it passes into the air sacs. Then you breathe it out.

! fun fact

Most humans can hold their breath for only 1 to 2 minutes. Bottlenose whales can hold their breath for 2 hours or longer.

Coughing and Sneezing

Tiny bits of dust and other material are always floating in the air. Some materials could make you sick if they got into your body.

The respiratory system helps keep these materials out of your body. For example, when you cough or sneeze you send a burst of air from your lungs out of your mouth or nose. The burst carries unwanted things out with it.

! fun fact

When you cough, air moves up the airway and out the mouth at a speed of about 100 miles (160 kilometers) per hour.

Breathing Is Automatic

You breathe without having to think about it. Your brain makes it happen automatically.

The brain sends a message to the **muscles** around the lungs. Muscles pull your chest walls out and down. This makes the space in your chest grow bigger. The lungs stretch to fill the bigger space, which allows air to flow inside. When the muscles relax, the space in your chest shrinks. This pushes air out of the lungs.

! fun fact

The left lung is slightly smaller than the right lung. This allows space for the heart.

When you exercise, your muscles need
extra oxygen for energy. Your brain makes
you breathe more often or more deeply.

Your breathing goes back to normal when you rest. It slows even more when you sleep. Even then, your respiratory system never stops working to fuel your cells and keep your body working.

Glossary

air sacs—tiny round pouches in the lungs where oxygen moves from the air into the blood; carbon dioxide moves from the blood to the air sacs.

blood vessels—tubes that carry blood throughout the body

bronchial tubes—tubes that branch out from the trachea and lead into the lungs; bronchial tubes carry air into and out of the lungs.

carbon dioxide—a waste material released by human cells; your blood carries carbon dioxide to your lungs and you breathe it out.

cells—the basic building blocks of living things

circulatory system—the body system made up of the heart, blood, and blood vessels; the circulatory system is responsible for transporting blood throughout the body.

lungs—the organs that take in air and supply oxygen to blood

muscle—a body part that can squeeze and produce force or motion

oxygen—a gas in air that human cells need to stay alive; you breathe in oxygen and your blood carries it to your cells.

trachea—the pipe that brings air to the lungs

To Learn More

AT THE LIBRARY
Houghton, Gillian. *Breath: The Respiratory System.*
New York: Powerkids Press, 2007.

Simon, Seymour. *Lungs: Your Respiratory System.*
New York: HarperCollins, 2007.

Taylor-Butler, Christine. *The Respiratory System.* New
York: Children's Press, 2008.

ON THE WEB
Learning more about the respiratory
system is as easy as 1, 2, 3.

1. Go to www.factsurfer.com.

2. Enter "respiratory system" into the search box.

3. Click the "Surf" button and you will see a list of
   related Web sites.

With factsurfer.com, finding more information is just a
click away.

Index

The images in this book are reproduced through the courtesy of: Sebastian Kaulitzki, front cover; Artiga Photo / Masterfile, p. 4; Jacek Chabraszewski, p. 6; Monkey Business Images, pp. 7, 11; Linda Clavel, diagrams, pp. 8-9, 11, 12; Jani Bryson, pp. 8-9; kristian sekulic, pp. 13, 20; eva serrabassa, pp. 14-15; Laura Johansen / Masterfile, pp. 16-17; Mandy Godbehear, pp. 18-19; Domenico Gelermo, p. 21.